What Helps the Most...

When Hope Is Hard to Find

101 Insights
From People Who Have Been There

Edited by Lisa O. Engelhardt

Abbey Pr
St. Meinrad, I

© 1996 St. Meinrad Archabbey
Published by One Caring Place
Abbey Press
St. Meinrad, Indiana 47577

Library of Congress Catalog Number
96-84538

ISBN 0-87029-294-3

The Scripture quotations contained herein are from
the New Revised Standard Version of the Bible,
© 1989 by the Division of Christian Education
of the National Council of the Churches of Christ
in the United States of America,
and are used by permission. All rights reserved.

Book design by Scott Wannemuehler

Printed in the United States of America

Dedication

To my friend, Joanne,
with whom I've shared
young hope and not-so-young hope,
borrowed hope and loaned hope,
lost hope and found hope.

Introduction

Hope is something we don't pay much attention to—until we realize it's gone. Sometimes it gushes out of a life punctured by pain. Other times it wears down through the slow erosion of chronic pain or problems.

At the moment we realize hope has left us, we realize how necessary it is. Hope is what gets us up in the morning and gets us to sleep at night—and gets us through in between. Hope keeps us from doing some desperate things and inspires us to do other desperate things. Hope is something solid and bright to hold on to when we feel ourselves being sucked into the black vacuum of despair.

But what *is* hope really and how do we get it back? Is it a feeling we can muster up through willpower? Is it a prize we can bargain for by praying really hard? Is it a blessing that rains down randomly? Is it something we already always have and we just need to realize this—like a scarecrow's brain, a tin man's heart, or a lion's courage?

What helps the most when hope is hard to find? This book offers insights into that question through a harmony of 101 voices. The common chord uniting these voices is their membership in "the great family of the heavy-hearted into which our grief has given us entrance," as Helen Keller puts it. These people are famous and not-so-famous, ancient and contemporary. They are saints and sports figures, entertainers and executives, a rabbi and an archbishop, great thinkers and those just struggling to get through another day.

The situations that have taught them how to hope are diverse—illness, disability, loss, depression, imprisonment, addiction, abuse, family problems, great personal suffering. Their perspectives on finding hope are rich and varied and sometimes paradoxical: Hope is found in holding on and letting go; helping oneself and leaning on others; crying and laughing; looking within and without.

In the mosaic of hope that emerges from these 101 pieces of personal truth, we discover, like clinical social worker Bonnie O. Miller, that "hope is both a gift and a choice. We ask for it and choose to act it. Hope is a way of being now, trusting in God's movement in the world....Hope is now, in the continually unfolding present—teaching us that something beyond ourselves is here."

May this little book help you to find the something beyond yourself that is real and solid and as close to you as your own heartbeat. May you find hope, choose hope, *be* hope now.

—Lisa O. Engelhardt

It helps the most to...

Trust

1. Anxiety in human life is what squeaking and grinding are in machinery that is not oiled. In life, trust is the oil.

—Henry Ward Beecher

2. The same everlasting Father who cares for you today will take care of you tomorrow and every day. Either he will shield you from suffering, or he will give you unfailing strength to bear it. Be at peace then and put aside all anxious thoughts and imaginations.

—St. Francis de Sales

3.   Ye fearful saints, fresh courage take,
The clouds ye so much dread
Are big with mercy and shall break
In blessings on your head.

—William Cowper

4.   I can't say what it is that has gradually dissolved this bitterness toward God. Time? My angry "prayers"? God's own workings? I only know that, little by little, God's goodness—visible in other people, in the world, in myself—became too apparent for me to ignore or deny. And I began to trust again.

    That, after all, is what it comes down to—trust. Trust that a life doesn't end with death. Trust that there really is some plan governing the seemingly random tragedies we suffer. Trust that our loved ones who have died are forever with God and that God is forever with us, too.

—Dr. Robert DiGiulio, in the CareNote *Losing Someone Close.*
His wife, oldest child, and in-laws were killed in a car accident.

5. The best prayer is to rest in the goodness of God, knowing that that goodness can reach right down to our lowest depths of need.

—Julian of Norwich

6. *Friday night, late*
Neither Luverne nor I have repeated the word our doctor uttered to us in his office today.

"Cancer," he had said. "Cancer in the prostate."

When we went to bed I found the hollow in my loved one's neck and burrowed my face there and felt his tears wetting my hair, and then I cried.

In my darkness I have searched for peace but found it not. Luverne is asleep now, but I cannot sleep. I'll warm some milk, read a while, crawl in bed again, and hope sleep will come.

Saturday morning, early
Dawn is slowly parting the lids of night. The birds outside are striking up their morning concerts. How can they sing? I wonder. Don't they know?

Saturday evening
My shower, usually so cheering, offered me no refreshment this morning. In the kitchen, making breakfast, I moved with difficulty, my legs so heavy I could scarcely put one in front of the other.

After breakfast I assembled all the boxes of

Christmas decorations. Opening the first one labeled "candles," I spied a strip of parchment lying on the bottom. Idly I lifted it out. On it Janet, during her high school years when she was designing wall plaques, had inscribed in calligraphy: "So give me the strength I need."

I stared at the words. I had found a prayer I could and would pray. Taking the paper, I taped it to the refrigerator door.

April 4
This morning I gently lifted the paper with my prayer from the refrigerator door and, putting it between two pieces of cardboard, stored it in the trunk of my memorabilia. Luverne is recovering, and the prospect for the future appears very hopeful. The help I have need-

ed all these weeks always has been just a prayer away.
—Mildred Tengbom, author

7. Capsized in open water, I prayed now in a way I
never had—though I had surely prayed before. A
glimpse of death opens the dimension of prayer and
bathes it with unprecedented light and clarity. Now
the matter of faith left the mainland of the rational:
Sheer sightless faith itself, adrift, no land in sight, perhaps became true, functioning faith for the first time,
and, doing so, acquired a power I had not felt before.
Prayer was uncontaminated by reason, defied reason.
—Lance Morrow, *Heart: A Memoir*

8. Some people imagine that hope is the highest degree
of optimism, a kind of super-optimism. I get the image

of someone climbing higher and higher to the most fanciful pinnacle of optimism, there to wave the little flag of hope. A far more accurate picture would be that hope happens when the bottom drops out of our pessimism. We have nowhere to fall but into the ultimate reality of God's motherly caring.

—Brother David Steindl-Rast, *Gratefulness, The Heart of Prayer*

9. Maybe the answers are, at least for now, too difficult to bear. Jesus said, "Blessed are those who mourn" not because he promised their questions would be answered but because he promised their hearts would be comforted.

When our hearts are broken and our eyes are blinded with tears, we don't need answers nearly as much as we need a father's lap to crawl onto and his shoulder where we can bury our face and cry....I'm not getting through the loss of my arm because I am a great coper. I'm getting through it because I have a father in heaven who is a great giver. *He* is where I find the grace. At the time I need strength, he puts it in my heart or provides it through someone who is close to me, whether that's a family doctor or simply a friend. I don't earn it. I don't deserve it. I don't bring it about. It's a gift. And that is how I am able to cope with the "tragic irony" of losing my arm.

—Dave Dravecky, *When You Can't Come Back: A Story of Courage & Grace.* Former all-star pitcher for the San Francisco Giants, Dravecky lost his pitching arm to cancer.

10. God hugs you. You are encircled by the arms of the mystery of God.

—Hildegard of Bingen

11. It was my faith that made it possible for me to cope positively with these two events. For forty-three years as a priest and twenty-nine as a bishop, I have counseled people to trust in the Lord, to believe that he would give them strength...but when I faced the traumas myself, I discovered that I *truly* believed it; that it was, indeed, part of my very being!

My faith gave me a perspective, a peace, a hope that enabled me to deal positively with the realities I was facing. I literally felt the presence of the Lord; it was as if he was saying to me: "I will not abandon you. I will walk with you and help you through all of this."

—Joseph Bernardin, Archbishop of Chicago.
In November 1993, a false charge of sexual impropriety was brought against him, which was later dismissed at his accuser's request.
Six months after this, the cardinal was diagnosed with pancreatic cancer.

12. Is God present or is he absent? Maybe we can say now that in the center of our sadness for his absence we can find the first signs of his presence. And that in the middle of our longings we discover the footprints of the one who has created them.

—Henri J. M. Nouwen,
Out of Solitude: Three Meditations on the Christian Life

13. *God within me, God without,*
How can I ever be in doubt?
I am the sower and the sown,
God's self unfolding and God's own.

—Runic saying

14. It *does* matter whether you say "yes" or "no" to life. For when you say "yes" your perceptions begin to

change. That which seems so senseless no longer seems quite so terrible. Soon an inner power is felt. A belief begins to emerge that, no matter what the odds, it is possible to move life forward....

What does it mean to "trust life"?

- Living in the present. Taking one day at a time.
- Pushing aside doubts that you can ever again be happy.
- Relying on friends. Asking them for comfort.
- Telling others how you feel: Lonely. Fearful. Hopeful.
- Affirming that you are good. Your intentions are good. Your past has been good. Your future will be good.

—Robert L. Veninga, *A Gift of Hope: How We Survive Our Tragedies*

15. Let the waves roar,
    Let the wind blow,

Let the world turn upside-down,
Let everything be in darkness, in smoke, in uproar,
Nothing can hurt you.
God is near.

—St. Francis de Sales

It helps the most to...

Hold On

16. Affliction…does not bereave of hope, but recruits hope. For affliction compels the person mercilessly to let go of everything else that he may learn to grasp the eternal and hang on to the eternal.

—Soren Kierkegaard

17. No one likes pain or sickness or difficulty or a sense of darkness and being alone. But if we can accept it as part of life and hold on to God…we shall emerge eventually toughened and strengthened.

—J. B. Phillips

18. Never think that God's delays are God's denials. Hold on; hold fast; hold out. Patience is genius.
—Comte Georges Louis Leclerc de Buffon

19. Hope is the thing with feathers
That perches in the soul
And sings the tune without the words
And never stops at all.

—Emily Dickinson

20. Give God time.

—The Koran

21. Nothing can make up for the absence of someone whom we love, and it would be wrong to try to find a substitute; we must simply hold out and see it through. That sounds very hard at first, but at the

same time it is a great consolation, for the gap, as long as it remains unfilled, preserves the bonds between us. It is nonsense to say that God fills the gap; God doesn't fill it, but on the contrary, keeps it empty and so helps us to keep alive our former communion with each other, even at the cost of pain.

—Dietrich Bonhoeffer

22. He did not say: You will not be troubled, you will not be belabored, you will not be disquieted; but He said: You will not be overcome.

—Julian of Norwich

23. When I was in pain, for years I prayed for the next doctor's appointment, the next treatment to miraculously free me from the grip of intolerable pain. My

anguish subsided when I started praying for the strength to bear it.

—Joanne Yount, recovered after seventeen years of pain

24. When Janice Hastings was told that she would have to have a radical mastectomy, which would leave her with two large scars, she thought about doing away with herself. "It was impossible to comprehend what was about to happen. I cried hysterically. I could not imagine what it would be like. It was so inconceivable that I was actually living this nightmare."

A week before her surgery she began to have suicidal thoughts. What kept her from doing it? Later she reflected on one important thing that helped: "One night I thumbed through the day's mail. I noticed a postcard sent by my best friend. He had written one

word on the postcard, scrawled in big letters: LIVE. Whenever I was tempted to harm myself I would look at that word and repeat it again and again and again: Live! Live! Live! I began to believe that I was not my body—*I was me.*
—Robert L. Veninga, *A Gift of Hope: How We Survive Our Tragedies*

25. Believe that life is worth living and your belief will help create the fact.

—William James

26. The One who is perfect dwells within and longs to heal and bring us to perfection. Pray for healing and look for it. And don't be surprised if it is your outlook which first needs healing. You must look into your heart and find a reason—however small—for living

and then realize that God created that reason, and
longs to help you live in wholeness and happiness.
—Susan Saint Sing,
in the CareNote *Finding God in Pain or Illness*

27. I had moved to Albuquerque, uprooting my life to
start over in the "Land of Enchantment" with my husband and hoping to establish a counseling practice in
the new locale. There was a lot of stress—selling our
house, buying a new home long distance, seeing my
son graduate and knowing he was leaving the nest as
he went off to college.

Three months after arriving, my husband was
diagnosed with prostate cancer. So, hardly settled in
and still not really knowing anyone, we went through
his surgery and recovery. Then came time for my

annual checkup. It was following a mammogram that I got the call telling me I had cancer. Despite a supportive, loving husband, the bottom dropped out of my already uncertain world. The momentum we had worked so hard to establish in terms of networking and building our practice came to a halt. I faced surgery, recovery, chemotherapy, and radiation. How would I work? I felt overwhelmed, frightened, and without hope for the future.

I called a friend, Christine, in Denver who came to Albuquerque to help see me through the surgery and recovery. What helped the most was her presence and a beautiful quilt she made for me with the inscription: "To comfort you, now and always!"

It was the nurturing message of comfort and the word "always" that gave me the strength to recognize that I was a survivor and I could make it through this experience. The word "always" hooked me to the future and moved me ahead of the immediate reality into the time beyond. Now, on a regular basis, I love to curl up under my "comfort quilt" and be nurtured…always!

—Rosemary Clarke, Ph.D.
She and her husband, Ric Solano, Ph.D., have developed
a program and counseling practice called CoupleSKILLS.

28. You have to suffer; not every day, but as a consequence of time….You'll live through it. You can't control suffering because if you try to avoid it then you kill rapture and joy. The two are inextricably linked. Joy never comes without suffering and therefore demands courage. For myself that means that if something terrible happens to me, I say to myself what my mother used to say to me, "Worse things have hap-

pened to nicer people." You'd be amazed at how that works.

—Rita Mae Brown, in *The Courage of Conviction*

29. Everything can be taken from a person but one thing: the last of human freedoms—to choose one's attitude in any given set of circumstances—to choose one's own way.

—Viktor Frankl

30. With the fearful strain that is on me night and day, if I did not laugh I should die.

—Abraham Lincoln

31. Let nothing disturb thee;
Let nothing dismay thee;
All things pass:

God never changes.
Patience attains
All that it strives for.
The one who has God
lacks nothing:
God alone suffices.

—St. Teresa of Avila

32. Yet the truth—and it is a great truth—is this: the supply of misery, pain, and suffering is unlimited, but so is the supply of pleasure, contentment, and fulfillment. It is we who do the rationing.

Ration no more! Capture wellness this instant! This instant is all there is. Live it!
—*Greg Anderson, The 22 Non-Negotiable Laws of Wellness: Feel, Think, and Live Better Than You Ever Thought Possible*

It helps the most to...

Let go

33. My friend, you belong to God. Let this reality color your entire existence. Give yourself up to God ceaselessly with every beat of your heart.

—St. Vincent de Paul

34. So often, we believe that we have come to a place that is void of hope and void of possibilities, only to find that it is the very hopelessness that allows us to hit bottom, give up our illusion of control, turn it over, and ask for help. Out of the ashes of our hopelessness comes the fire of our hope.

—Anne Wilson Schaef

35. There is a ritual that I find helpful in any time of spiritual darkness. Pick a place that gives you solace. It could be a waterfall in the woods where the rhythm of the cascading water blends into the silence of the woods to bring you peace. It could be a huge craggy rock jutting out into the ocean, a place where the ocean beats the shore with an urgency that brings you back to the awe of the universe. Whatever place speaks to you, go and listen!

Speak to God telling him how you feel. You start the dialogue. God will be listening. Be honest about your despair, your fears, even your anger.

Then, in a ceremonial prayer, give your problem to God. Think of your problem being lifted up from you by a power so great it can regulate the tides of the ocean, or order the universe. Know that your problem is being received by God. Become willing to let him do for you what you cannot do for yourself!

Watch your problem go; feel its weight being lifted from you. Do this as many times as necessary. Then, thank God for taking your problem away and for the relief you feel. Cry—let all the sadness go! God is in charge now and you are free from the darkness that has followed you.

Later, even when you can't be in that special location, transport yourself there in your mind and give your darkness to God. Light will filter in, bit by bit, like the awakening of a new day. Darkness lifts and a new hope is born.

—Christine A. Adams, teacher and author

36. At every point in the human journey we find that we have to let go in order to move forward; and letting go means dying a little. In the process we are being created anew, awakened afresh to the source of our being.
—Kathleen R. Fischer

37. We want to be healed, we want to mend the broken pieces of our souls, we want the cup of suffering to pass from us, yet it is not to be. Instead, we are to ask for one thing only—the surrender of our beings to God. With this surrender, which comes of grace, comes the wholeness that is unattainable through human effort. With this surrender comes the light that guides us on the path of the spirit; and with this surrender comes a faith in, not a God of rescue and restoration, but a God who would love and live in us, even

through our trials and tribulations.

—Adolfo Quezada,
Through the Darkness: Glimmers of Hope

38. I do not want to die without leaving a record of my belief that suffering can be overcome. For I do believe it. What must one do? One must submit. Do not resist. Take it. Be overwhelmed. Accept it fully. Make it part of life.

—Mildred Tengbom,
Why Waste Your Illness? Let God Use It for Growth

39. When I was diagnosed with MS twenty years ago, I could tell people I had the disease quite easily, probably because I did not know what was in store for me. Each time my MS strips away another part of my body,

I cry a bit more, and it takes me a little longer to say to myself I have MS.

It reminds me of wedding vows. On a couple's wedding day, they vow to love and obey for better or for worse forever. Each year, because of financial troubles, children, and just the day-to-day trials of everyday life, the reality of saying those vows becomes more difficult.

Acknowledging that you have a chronic disease can be a freeing event in your life. Some people can say it all at once, and others gradually, and still others can never say it. What it seems to do for me is to let me be honest about my limitations, and then I can go on with my life. For better or for worse.

—Karen J. Zielinski, O.S.F., head of the communications office for the Sisters of St. Francis of Sylvania, Ohio

40. We are healed of a suffering only by experiencing it to the full.

—Marcel Proust

41. Truly it is allowed to weep. By weeping, we disperse our wrath; and tears go through the heart, even like a stream.

—Ovid

42. Look upon each day that comes as a challenge, as a test of courage. The pain will come in waves, some days worse than other, for no apparent reason. Accept the pain. Do not suppress it. Never attempt to hide grief from yourself.

—Daphne Du Maurier

43. What is the greatest evil of suffering? Not the suffer-

ing itself but our rebellion against it, the state of interior revolt which often accompanies it.

—Jean Grou

44. My daughter Aimee was nineteen years old when she dived into an above-ground pool and broke her neck. The next shock wave came when the doctors delivered their diagnosis: Aimee has a spinal cord injury that would leave her paralyzed from the neck down for the rest of her life.

Hope is all-important in overcoming your bewilderment and pain. Hope is not false; it is real. When the pain is fresh, hope is all you have. It's like God's hand on your shoulder, buoying you above this unbelievable reality until you reach the shore of acceptance. The magic, wonderful thing about hope is that it gradually transforms your prayers from the unattainable to the attainable, gaining your approval in bits and pieces along the way.

My prayers for Aimee slowly evolved from "Please heal her physically" to "Please give her acceptance and give me the strength to take care of her." Those prayers have been answered.

—Candice Sackuvich, in the CareNote
When a Loved One's Accident or Illness Changes Your Life

45. To hope is to create a sacred space, a space of possibility, in which the goodness of the Universe can express itself. The stance we adopt in that sacred space is one of readiness, openness, and non-attachment to a particular outcome.

—Joan Borysenko,
Fire in the Soul: A New Psychology of Spiritual Optimism

46. About eighteen months ago my entire belief system came crashing to the ground. Systemic lupus caused the blood supply in my hip to be damaged to the extent that my hip was actually threatened. I finally agreed to surgical intervention designed specifically to restore the hip's blood supply. If nothing was done I faced the immediate chance that my hip would literally crumble.

Well, surgery failed and my hip did break. That began an eighteen-month saga that is not quite over to this day. Operation after operation ensued. Needless to say, it was a life-threatening and terrifying time for me.

In short, I was one terrified lady. And so I prayed. But this time my prayers were different. I did a quantum leap from casual praying to an almost instant awareness of God's power. For the first time in my life

I was ready and willing to turn my life over to God. If there were problems in the operating room or in intensive care, I knew he was there, watching over me. I felt peace. I knew, once and forever, that God is a loving and caring God, and whatever decision he makes will be the right one.

I know God now in a whole different way than I did before. I willingly place my life in his hands—every day, every night. I always have hope. I have choices in my life as I always have, and one of them, now and forever, is believing that God walks with me, always holding my hand.

—Sefra Kobrin Pitzele, author

It helps the most to...

Help yourself

47. And if God does not help me to go on, then I shall have to help God.
—An Interrupted Life: The Diaries of Etty Hillesum, 1941-1943

48. Whatsoever we beg of God, let us also work for it.
—Jeremy Taylor

49. When I was young, I learned to sail a catboat on Manhasset Bay. I remember, as we went skimming along the water before a gusty wind, I yelled worriedly to the old expert who was my teacher, "If the wind

keeps blowing in this direction, how do we get back?"
"Wind don't matter a darn," he replied. "Wind can
blow how it likes. It's the set of your sail makes the
difference."

It's how we react to the things that happen to us
that "makes the difference." If we see life as threaten-
ing and dangerous, we will be afraid. If we see it as
basically good, we will feel comfortable. Yet it is both,
and it is with the reality of its wholeness that we must
live.

—Dorothy F. Edgerton, *Walk On in Peace*

50. Call on God, but row away from the rocks.

—Indian Proverb

51. Now is no time to think of what you do not have.

Think of what you can do with what there is.

—Ernest Hemingway

52. Ultimately you must learn to comfort yourself. No matter how many people are around during the day, reality can be very hard to face in the loneliness of the night.

Keep up your self-esteem. Be kind to yourself. Hug yourself if you can't find anybody to hug you. Don't feel cursed if you have a disease with a foul name. Don't think of yourself as worthless or worth less because you've been stricken.

I really believe my fighting spirit meant the difference between life and death for me. My nurses told me that once when I was delirious, I pounded on the bed rails yelling, "Come on, Hirshel!" I was cheering

myself on like my wife and daughters cheered for me
when I ran the New York City Marathon.
—Rabbi Hirshel Jaffe, recounting his battle with hairy-cell leukemia,
in the CareNote *Hanging On to Hope Through Serious Illness*

53. Be patient with everyone, but above all with yourself.
I mean, do not be disturbed because of your imperfec-
tions, and always rise up bravely from a fall. I'm glad
that you make daily a new beginning; there is no better means of progress in the spiritual life than to be
continually beginning afresh.

—St. Francis de Sales

54. The natural healing force within each one of us is the
greatest force in getting well.

—Hippocrates

55. Silence is the strength of our interior life....If we fill
our lives with silence, then we will live in hope.
—Thomas Merton

56. I suffer from depression. Sometimes the emotional fog
rolls in, seemingly from nowhere, and I'm enshrouded.
Hope leave town and takes joy and meaning with her.

This condition can last awhile and the pain gets
close to overwhelming. The color goes out of life; even
enjoying myself feels flat and painful. For so long I
knew of nothing else to do but hunker down and
endure. By and by a day would come when I would
awake and, just as mysteriously as it descended, the
fog would have lifted.

Today I have come to know the power of creativity
to lift me above the fog. Whether it's dabbling in oil

painting, crafting a poem, baking a pie, writing a long
letter to a dear friend, singing my heart out (at church
or along with an "oldies" station), brainstorming with
the creative people I work with, constructing a jumbo
sign to proclaim the new parish renewal program, or
trying to outpun my wife and daughters, throwing my
energies into some creative pursuit will more often
than not redeem me from hopelessness. Creativity is
nothing more than playing, and for me, play is what
the doctor ordered. I have come to believe that playing
(creating with abandon) is participating in the life and
work of God our Creator. And while I am doing that,
the meaning, the joy, and, yes, the hope creep back to
see what all the fun is about.

—Tom McGrath,
editorial director of Claretian Publications

57. The best remedy for those who are afraid, lonely, or unhappy is to go outside, somewhere where they can be quite alone with the heavens, nature, and God. Because only then does one feel that all is as it should be and that God wishes to see people happy, amidst the simple beauty of nature. As long as this exists, and it certainly always will, I know that then there will always be comfort for every sorrow, whatever the circumstances may be.

—Anne Frank

58. Help thy brother's boat across, and lo! thine own has reached the shore.

—Hindu proverb

59. When your burden is heaviest, you can always light-

en a little some other burden. At the times when you cannot see God, there is still open to you this sacred possibility, to *show* God; for it is the love and kindness of human hearts through which the divine reality comes home to men, whether they name it or not. Let this thought, then, stay with you: there may be times when you cannot find help, but there is no time when you cannot give help.

—George S. Merriam

60. When you find yourself overpowered by melancholy, the best way is to go out and do something kind to somebody.

—John Keble

61. Trouble not thyself by pondering life in its entirety....

Rather, as each occasion arises in the present, put this question to thyself: "Where lies the unbearable, unendurable part of this task?"…Next recall to mind that neither past nor future can weigh thee down, only the present. And the present will shrink to littleness if thou but set it apart, assign it its boundaries, and then ask thy mind if it avail not to bear even this!

—Marcus Aurelius

62. The man who removed mountains began by carrying away small stones.

—Chinese proverb

63. My perfectionist point of view prohibited me from realizing that improvement could be made effectively in increments. To my mind, it had always been all or

....nothing. My issues were black and white—there was no room for gray. Now a whole new realm of possibilities had opened up for me. Clearly, the mountain still had to be moved—there was no getting around it. But it could be moved truckload by truckload, or even, if necessary, tablespoon by tablespoon! If a thimble were all I could carry, then, with God's help, I would move that monstrosity one thimbleful at a time!

> —Cherry Boone O'Neill, *Starving for Attention.*
> A singer and dancer and the daughter of
> recording star Pat Boone, O'Neill waged an
> agonizing battle against anorexia nervosa.

64. Never bear more than one kind of trouble at a time. Some people bear three—all they have had, all they have now, and all they expect to have.

> —Edward Everett Hale

65. If you are distressed by anything external, the pain is not due to the thing itself, but to your estimate of it; and this you have the power to revoke at any moment.
—Marcus Aurelius

66. It is essential to distinguish between what you can and cannot control. If a crisis is beyond your control, you can deflect its impact by taking on a new challenge. Choose a new task to master, like learning to swim or learning a foreign language, to reassure yourself that you are still the master of your own fate....When all else fails, play a new game.
—Dr. Kenneth R. Pelletier,
Sound Mind, Sound Body: A New Model for Lifelong Health

67. Have courage for the great sorrows of life and

patience for the small ones; and when you have labori-
ously accomplished your daily task, go to sleep in
peace. God is awake.

—Victor Hugo

It helps the most to...

Lean on others

68. Without friends the world is but a wilderness....There is no man that imparteth his joys to his friends, but he joyeth the more; and no man that imparteth his griefs to his friends, but he grieveth the less.

—Francis Bacon

69. Two weeks had passed since my doctor had said that phrase so many of us dread: "It's cancer." I turned on my family who I was sure couldn't understand. My faith seemed to be failing me. I couldn't pray and this made me even angrier. Where was God when I needed him the most? Why had this happened to me?

I sat there, my arms locked around my legs, head on my knees. The doorbell rang. There stood Marty, a friend who taught with me. He'd had cancer six years earlier. All I could think of was, "I'm not ready for this."

He didn't *tell* me anything. He just said, "You may not be ready yet, but if you want to talk, I'm here." Until that moment I had not let anyone hug me. I guess I didn't trust being vulnerable. But something happened as Marty stood there asking nothing of me. I reached out and as he held me I sobbed, "I'm so afraid."

During the next hour or two I spewed out all the conflicting emotions that I hadn't been able to share even with those closest to me. I *knew* he understood and that no matter what I said, he would not judge me. I felt comforted. My healing had begun.

As I reflect on that day eight years ago, I wonder why I was able to respond to Marty and not to others who reached out to me. Part of it was timing, but most of it was that I knew if I refused to speak with him it would be okay. He wasn't there to talk *to* me, to convince me I'd be okay, or to *tell* me what I should be doing or thinking. He was simply *present to me*. He offered himself to me in love, no strings attached.

Through his gift of himself, I found what I thought I had lost: faith in myself and faith in my God. Being able to connect with someone who understood and accepted me as I was gave me strength. Today I know that God was with me even when I doubted the most. He has sent many people to me but when I felt lost and alone with my illness, he sent Marty as a gift to me, a gift of hope that allowed me to face my illness and discover a peace I had not believed possible.

—Marianna K. Neal, a recently retired high school Spanish teacher who works as a free-lance writer

70. Stay connected to others. You need their presence, their support, their concern, their listening, their hugs.

—Karen Katafiasz, *Grief Therapy*

71. A myth from East India has been my greatest source of hope during dark times caused by progressive multiple sclerosis and a severe hearing loss.

Many years ago, a child was born in India. His parents knew that their son was extraordinary and that someday he would save his people from extinction. The boy grew up, mindful of his destiny.

One day, when he was about nineteen, he and his brother were walking by a lagoon. As they approached, they saw a huge snake thrashing about. This snake, over the years, left nothing but destruction in its path. It threatened the survival of the tribe.

The young man turned to his brother and said, "My hour has come. It is time for me to save my people." He jumped into the water and the snake immediately wrapped itself around him and began choking the life out of him. He was near death when his brother cried out from shore: "Brother, remember who you are. Remember the power within you." Immediately the young man was able to overpower the snake, kill it, save himself and his people.

Who are the sisters and brothers on the sidelines of your life who can remind you to plug into this

Divine Power within you? Have you asked them to be your "cheerleaders" in the game of life? Do you listen to their hope-filled challenge?

—Mary Kraemer, O.S.F.

72. When it seems that our sorrow is too great to be borne, let us think of the great family of the heavy-hearted into which our grief has given us entrance, and inevitably, we will feel about us their arms, their sympathy, their understanding.

—Helen Keller

73. Working in a mental health hospital, I had seen major depression many times, but always from the outside. Because of a profound personal loss, I was now experiencing it firsthand. And how it felt from the inside. I

had lost all hope and my inner pain was unbearable. I felt walled off from my husband, family, and closest friends. Pleasure in the smallest daily tasks and occurrences had vanished quite suddenly.

Stripped of any semblance of my former self-confidence, I found it difficult to function. Merely making a phone call at work seemed to be an insurmountable task. Folding a load of laundry took an hour sometimes. But usually the dirty clothes just laid on the floor around the bed from where I fixed my eyes on the ceiling. For months I struggled with the bleakness.

I resisted help because I was afraid of admitting that I needed help like the hundreds of others who checked into our facility each year. My fear of co-workers talking about me bordered on true paranoia.

Then one day I realized that they already knew. A

close buddy at work came into my office and handed me a small box. She said nothing, just briefly hugged my shoulder as she stood next to me.

Inside was a small porcelain object. It was a clown with a sad, yet peaceful expression on its face. I read the note attached. It recounted how she had watched me fade in the months before but how she knew things would get better.

"Borrow my optimism for awhile," was how the note ended. She had given me a bit of her hope for my future in that small chipboard container.

I did not feel better right away, but that day I began to see the possibilities for healing. Finally I decided to get the assistance I needed. Medication helped get me moving physically. I received counsel-ing, in another town, still afraid of my co-workers finding out my secrets.

Recently after a move, I found an overlooked unpacked box. I absentmindedly loosened the packing tissue as my daughter skipped into the room. When that clown gently fell on my lap, a flood of tears welled up in me. Soon I was sobbing.

"Why are you sad, Mommy?" asked my precious four-year-old. Then she snatched the clown away with all the impulsiveness so characteristic of her age. "Oh, what's this? Can I have it?"

"It's a bit of confidence in tomorrow," I said, praying she would never really understand why we sometimes need symbols of our regained hope.

—Clair Bradshaw, R.N., free-lance writer

74. Our community is also helpful. Don't let your pride

keep your church, social, or government community
from helping you. Go to them. This may be their way
of serving God and their fellow man. Don't deny them
this opportunity. Rest in the strength of your friends.
—Mary Lou Betzweiser, who at age 42 found herself
a widow with eight minor children and little money

It helps the most to...

Remember love

75. When everything is dark, when we are surrounded by despairing voices, when we do not see any exits, then we can find salvation in a remembered love, a love which is not simply a recollection of a bygone past but a living force which sustains us in the present. Through memory, love transcends the limits of time and offers hope at any moment of our lives.

—Henri Nouwen

76. Before I left, I had a parlor with the abbess again. I had to know how to get over all the stupid suffering.

She said that the way to get rid of an inferior suffering is to accept a bigger one.

But why would anyone want to do that?

She said, "You have to love very much. You begin by remembering, Patricia. And when you remember all, what remains is love."…Remembering is the root of hope.

—Patricia Neal, *As I Am: An Autobiography.*
Actress Patricia Neal suffered the brain-damaging
injury of her baby son, the death of her young daughter,
three near-fatal strokes, and a devastating divorce.

77. After that, we only really talked with Alex of two things: her life, and what we could guess of death. It didn't seem to be the time for small talk, when your child was dying.

So we brought up as many people as Alex knew and loved that we could recall. We talked of the things she had done with them, and of the joys she had given them, and they her. We talked of all the places she had been and of all the wonderful things we had done together. We talked about her school and about her room and her house...and we even talked about the hospital and all her friends there. We talked about all the things Alex liked....Then we talked about the Broadway shows she had seen, and Benny Hill, who made her laugh, and all the dancing that she loved. Well, what we talked about was love. Love, love, love, Alex. We kept saying it.

—Frank Deford, *Alex: The Life of a Child.*
An author and sports writer, Deford lost his
daughter, Alex, to cystic fibrosis at the age of eight.

78. And time remembered is grief forgotten,
And frosts are slain and flowers begotten,
And in green underwood and cover
Blossom by blossom the spring begins.
—Algernon Charles Swinburne

79. …Memory nourishes the heart, and grief abates.
—Marcel Proust

80. Healing is knowing that forgiveness is the key to happiness and offers me everything that I want. Healing is knowing that the only reality in the universe is love, and that love is the most important healer known to the world.

—Gerald Jampolsky,
"Living and Loving One Second at a Time," in *Healers on Healing*

81. I kept trying to make amends to my family by saying I didn't understand how a person as intelligent as I could be such a total failure and a mess, do this to them, embarrass them this way. The emphasis was still on me and what I had done wrong.

I had to learn to forgive myself if I expected them to forgive me. And I couldn't forgive myself until I could believe God had forgiven me.

The Lord's Prayer says, "Forgive us our trespasses, as we forgive those who trespass against us." That was the beginning.

—Betty Ford, *Betty: A Glad Awakening.*
The former First Lady of the United States
suffered from alcoholism and drug addiction.

82. Then I had to make the choice to forgive myself. I had

done so many embarrassing things, so many unkind things. But I had to stop beating myself up about them. It was very personal—sort of a spiritual high colonic. And once I had done it, I was able to work more honestly on forgiving those who had hurt me when I was younger....I believe that bitterness is counterproductive, so in an almost selfish way it was important for me to forgive—to truly forgive. And I honest-to-God believe that I would be dead if I had hung on to all of the rage and bitterness that it was possible for me to have.

—Patty Duke, *A Brilliant Madness: Living With Manic-Depressive Illness*

83. I have found the paradox that if I love until it hurts, then there is no hurt, but only more love.

—Mother Teresa

84. I never dreamed such a tragedy could happen in my family. The Friday-night shootings that I read about in the paper on Saturday mornings always made me feel depressed. But three years ago, the violence really hit home when my brother Claudio became one of the innocent victims.

I had turned to God in my greatest hour of need, praying desperately that my wounded brother's life would be saved. Instead, Claudio died at age thirty-three, leaving behind his wife and two young daughters. For many months, my heart was full of hurt, fear, and anger toward God.

Even though I could not see or feel the presence of God during my darkest hours, I believe God was present in the family and friends who surrounded me. Embrace God's presence when you embrace your family and friends. Listen for the whisper of Love in the emptiness of your wounded heart. Know that no one truly journeys alone. Reach out your hand and you will find it enfolded in God's.

—Annabella Fantasma,
in the CareNote *Searching for God When You Lose Someone Close*

85. I learned it is not enough to passively carry a cross; you must pick it up, fight with it, deal with its weight, and, finally, love it.

—Antoinette Bosco, *The Pummeled Heart: Finding Peace Through Pain*. Bosco's son and daughter-in-law were murdered.

86. Winter. I hate cold, dark days. My winter began with the doctor's chilling diagnosis: "You have multiple myeloma...cancer." I walked through the valley of denial, anger, fear. To survive this harsh winter I

blanketed my spirit with faith.

Spring is hope. I wrote specific goals for recovery in my journal. God touched my life through the prayers of Jewish neighbors and Christian friends. Children encouraged me. Hope is confidence in God, a reason to live.

Summer is warmth and adventure. My wife's love and laughter lightened my burdens. I wrote notes and telephoned friends who needed to know that they were loved in their pain, grief, and loneliness. God's love is a gift to be shared.

Fall is change. After two years in remission, the cancer returned. I push myself to use my mind, to exercise, to keep praying and visualizing my recovery. The Chinese teach us, "When you are ill, do not focus on being cured. Find your center." So I keep trying to return to Christ, my Center.

Pain is a required course in life; misery is an elective. I am discovering how to grow in grace through suffering. Knowing Jesus Christ, being loved, and encouraging others makes life meaningful.

The gifts of faith, hope, and love are for all seasons.

—Joe Strother, a retired Baptist minister

87. I do not believe that sheer suffering teaches. If suffering alone taught, all the world would be wise, since everyone suffers. To suffering must be added mourning, understanding, patience, love, openness, and the willingness to remain vulnerable.

—Anne Morrow Lindbergh

It helps the most to...

Seek meaning

88. All suffering prepares the soul for vision.
—Martin Buber

89. You begin to see there is a future. And as the love and support and friendship of family and friends and people around the world, as all these things came to me and I realized their value, it [made me think], man, am I lucky. I am so lucky, it's unbelievable....

You also gradually discover, as I'm discovering, that your body is not you and the mind and the spirit must take over. And that's the challenge as you move from obsessing about "Why me?" and "It's not fair" and "When will I move again?" and all of those things and move into, "Well, what is the potential?"…We experience genuine joy being alive, because every moment means more. Every moment is more intense and valuable than it ever was….

You can say either the universe is totally random and it's just molecules colliding all the time and, you know, it's totally chaos and that our job is to make sense of chaos, or you can say sometimes things happen for a reason and your job is to discover the reason. But either way, I do see meaning and opportunity and that has made all the difference.

—Christopher Reeve, in an interview with
Barbara Walters on *20/20*. Actor Reeve was
paralyzed from the shoulders down after
a fall in a horseback riding competition.

90. To find God in life's hard, sharp, heavy, or blunt places is really to find God—not just warm generic feelings regarding pleasant, divine things, but God. And more: to look for God amidst what seems life's wreckage and rubble is to assert the fundamental religious truth that life—all life—means something.

—Michael Graham, S.J.,
"Finding God in *These* Things," *Xavier*, Fall 1994

91. Once a week one of the orphanage staff took Sarah to her room for special instructions about sex....On the bed at the foot of the crucifix, an attendant raped Sarah....In her mind she cried, she prayed, she pleaded for help from the "God on the cross." Each week she suffered. Each week the "God on the cross" did nothing but hang there and watch....

Many years later she began to understand where God had been when she was raped...."When I was being raped, God had come down off that cross and was in me. That is where God was. He was a little girl being raped, being raped with me. God was within me all that time and I didn't even know it."...

This offered Sarah a new hope—the hope of a God who was not just over her, greater than her. It was the hope of a God who was with her, a part of what she was enduring, including her powerlessness over people and circumstances.

—Horace O. Duke, *Where Is God When Bad Things Happen?*

92. It is the nature of grace always to fill spaces that have been empty.

—Goethe

93. I knew my father was dying (advanced cancer), and yet my wife was pregnant, and we took this as sort of a "consolation prize" from God. Yes, we were going to lose a much-loved father at age seventy, but we were going to gain a much-longed-for child. Isn't that the way God worked?

I'm a good person. We did all the right things. And yet my totally innocent father suffered cruelly and long with cancer, and we had another miscarriage. It made no sense to me to be praying and not have our prayers answered.

What helped was doing a lot of reading, praying, and listening to people who said what happened might have had a higher *purpose*, but what happened wasn't something God *wanted*—especially the suffering. It helped for me to read these words: "If logic tells you there is no [loving] God, don't give up on God, give up on *logic*." I needed to see that just because it would have made good logical *sense* for God to give us this child instead of a miscarriage, this didn't mean it was time to give up on God.

So, instead of looking for a God of power and might who would "fix" things, I started looking for a God of love and consolation who would *really* fix things. The answer that time has shown me…is that God answers prayers in God's way, not our way, and in God's time frame, not ours. This revelation came through loud and clear in time: Our God is a God of love and care and comfort and compassion, not only a "John Wayne" God of *power* and *might* who comes to our rescue at the big shootout.

—Linus Mundy, publisher of One Caring Place/Abbey Press. Mundy and his wife suffered three miscarriages, the final one occurring just two months before his father died.

94. I want to beg you as much as I can...to be patient toward all that is unsolved in your heart and to try to love the questions themselves....Do not now seek answers which cannot be given you because you would not be able to live them. And the point is to live everything. *Live* the questions now. Perhaps you will then gradually, without noticing it, live along some distant day into the answer....

—Rainer Maria Rilke

95. To one who waits all things reveal themselves, so long as you have the courage not to deny in the darkness what you have seen in the light.

—Coventry Patmore

96. We have sorrow so we can understand joy; failure so we can know success; pain, so we can relish pleasure. Somehow, built into the mystery of this duality is a blueprint for growth that has the potential for shaping us into who God wants us to be.

—Antoinette Bosco, *The Pummeled Heart*

97. "It takes a long time [to become Real]. That's why it doesn't often happen to people who break easily, or have sharp edges, or who have to be carefully kept. Generally, by the time you are Real, most of your hair has been loved off, and your eyes drop out and you get loose in the joints and very shabby. But these things don't matter at all, because once you are Real you can't be ugly, except to people who don't understand."

—Margery Williams, *The Velveteen Rabbit*

98. So we do not lose heart. Even though our outer nature is wasting away, our inner nature is being renewed day by day. For this slight momentary affliction is preparing us for an eternal weight of glory beyond all measure, because we look not at what can be seen but at what cannot be seen; for what can be seen is temporary, but what cannot be seen is eternal.

—2 Corinthians 4:16-18

99. And life is eternal and love is immortal, and death is only a horizon, and a horizon is nothing, save the limit of our sight.

—Attributed to Bede Jarrett

100. When you see through the fog for an instant and understand, even briefly, what good is and how God is connected with it, that cannot help but put a perspective on the things you perceive as problems. You discover multiple ways in which you've been numb. In that brief moment, you feel that God is in heaven and all is right with the world.

—Singer/songwriter Mark Heard, "Daring to Hope,"
The Other Side, Nov.-Dec. 1992. Heard died of heart failure
August 16, 1992, at the age of forty-one.

101. All shall be well, and all shall be well, and all manner of thing shall be well.

—Julian of Norwich

Acknowledgments

8. Reprinted from *Gratefulness, The Heart of Prayer* by Brother David Steindl-Rast, © by Brother David Steindl-Rast. Used by permission of Paulist Press.

9. Taken from *When You Can't Come Back* by Dave and Jan Dravecky. Copyright © 1992 by Dave and Jan Dravecky. Used by permission of Zondervan Publishing House.

12. Excerpted from *Out of Solitude: Three Meditations on the Christian Life* by Henri J. M. Nouwen. Copyright 1974 by Ave Maria Press, Notre Dame, IN 46556. Used with permission of the publisher.

23. Reprinted with permission of Joanne Yount, Executive Director, The Vulvar Pain Foundation, Post Office Drawer 177, Graham, NC 27253.

32. Quote from page 119 from *The 22 (Non-Negotiable) Laws of Wellness* by Greg Anderson. Copyright © 1995 by Greg Anderson. Reprinted by permission of HarperCollins Publisher, Inc.

38. Reprinted from *Why Waste Your Illness?* by Mildred Tengbom, copyright © 1984 Augsburg Publishing House. Used by permission of Augsburg Fortress.

Special thanks to all the generous spirits who shared their personal stories in this book.

Titles in the *What Helps the Most* Series

When Hope Is Hard to Find

When You Lose Someone Close